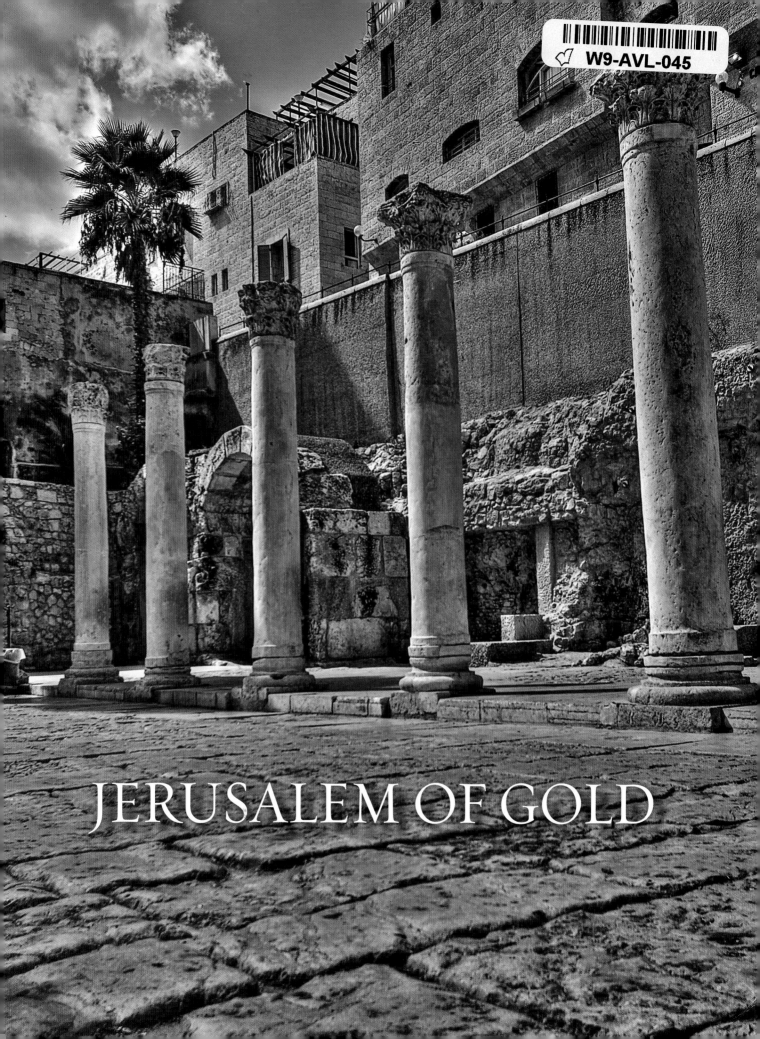

JERUSALEM OF GOLD

Dedication

My Jerusalem, I am honored and so grateful for having my
three princesses being born in your land.
They are the best gift this city could have ever given to me,
along with the redemption from my Lord and King, Yeshua Ben Yoseph.
I will love you Liel Adriana, Tahel Violeta and Hallel Andrea forever.

Contents

I am grateful to all those who assisted in the reviewing of this book especially Cariño Casas

Edited, Photographed, Written and Published by:
Marcos Enrique Ruiz Rivero II (AVIEL)

Design by : THINK AND DESIGN "Design & Printing Services"

ISBN: 978-965-7747-07-0

Marcos Enrique Ruiz Rivero II (AVIEL)
Mobile +972 (0)546 711 141
E-mail aviel_is.superguide@yahoo.com
Website: http://israelsuperguide.com

flickr.com/avielsuperguidephotography

Aviel is Superguide

INTRODUCTION

Jerusalem, my Jerusalem of gold. How many times have I not heard of you, how many times have I not read about you? Now I can finally see you, I can walk your streets, I can smell your scent, I can hear you...

Throughout history, millions of pilgrims have visited the holy city and many more have wanted to see her. Now it is your turn to discover what you have long heard of her and to experience for yourself, to walk her streets and feel her history.

What is it about Jerusalem that everyone wants to possess, conquer, destroy and rebuild her? It is her spell, enclosed within her walls, which makes everyone who visits her miss her and keep her in their memories.

When do we first hear about you, Jerusalem?

Before the Bible was written we already knew about you, for archaeology shows that you have been inhabited for at least 5,000 years. The Execration texts, written in the nineteenth century BCE spoke of you; el-Amarna letters of the fourteenth century BCE spoke of you again.

Finally, you arose in the tenth century BCE and became the eternal capital of the united kingdom under the leadership of King David. Despite the separation of Israel in the north, you continued to be the capital of Judea. You survived the siege of the Assyrians in 702 BCE but fell in 586 BCE when, sadly, you were looted, burned and destroyed by the Babylonians.

1

Consequently, after the Persians conquered Babylon in 539 BCE, you did not rise as capital of the entire empire but, at least, as the capital of the Persian province Yehud.

Under the conquest of the Greeks, led by Alexander the Great in the fourth century BCE, you no longer remained the capital of the province, yet you remained the center of Jewish worship. When Alexander died, his generals and successors (Ptolemy and Seleucid) not only fought to gain control over you but the entire region around you as well, until in 164 BCE your temple was cleansed and dedicated to your God. Years later, under the direction of the Hasmonean kings, you became not only the capital of a province once again, but the capital of an independent Jewish kingdom.

Sadly, your leaders, blinded in their quest for power, caused you to fall into the hands of another empire. In 64 BCE Rome annexed you to its vast empire and you passed from hand to hand, between Rome and her puppet Herod the Great and governors including Pontius Pilate. Your temple and your glory were destroyed again by the Romans in the year 70 CE.

Even when your walls were rebuilt by the Empress Eudocia in the fifth century CE, that did not keep you from being dominated by a new religion. In 638 CE you were conquered by Umar ibn Al-Khattab and his Islamic regime.

In 1099 CE, the Crusaders from Europe reached you and, with them, a new stage of your history began. Once again you became the capital of a new kingdom, under the leadership of European Christian kings, a period that lasted only until 1187 CE when the same were defeated by Muslims in the region known as the Horn of Hattin. Again you fell into the hands of Islam, through the Ayubids, and after them the Mamluks followed. Then you endured 400 years under Ottoman rule until you were relieved in 1917 during World War I. After that you lived under the British mandate until 1948 when, sadly, you were defiled by civil war. Consequently, you were split between the kingdom of Jordan and the reborn state of Israel, becoming once again the capital of an independent Jewish state. This event harkened back to the days of the Hasmonean kings of Judah. Within a few decades, in 1967, the Six-Day War reunited East and West Jerusalem.

Today you are not only the world center of the three predominant religions in the Middle East, but millions of visitors enter through your gates to draw closer to you. They can feel your roots and the power of God, or perhaps in your streets they simply feel your ancient history in all its glory.

As a guide, archaeologist, theologian and photographer, my goal is to convey Jerusalem's significance, identity, spirituality and beauty. In your visit, I invite you to walk her paths and feel her energy, which will mark you forever. No wonder she is called Jerusalem, the Eternal City, Jerusalem of Gold.

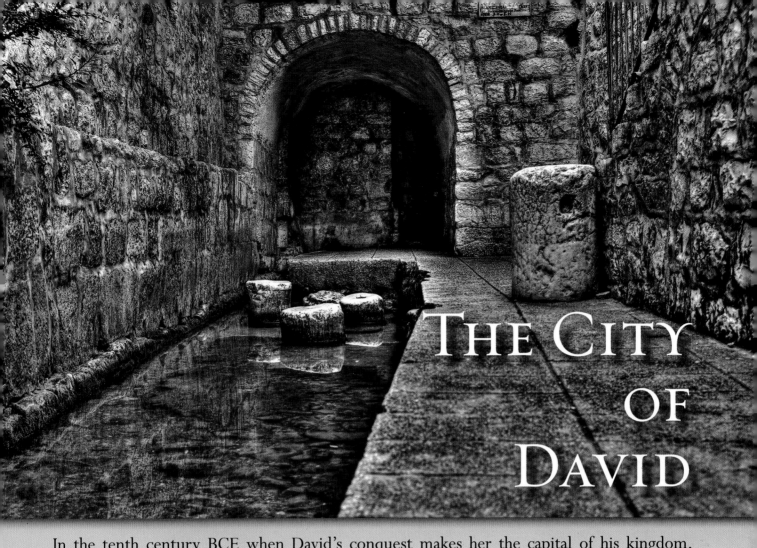

THE CITY OF DAVID

In the tenth century BCE when David's conquest makes her the capital of his kingdom, Jerusalem already had at least 2,000 years of habitation. From there, he and his son Solomon reigned as kings of Judah and their descendants until the Babylonian destruction in 586 BCE.

The City of David has become the most excavated archaeological site in the world, and thanks to the discovery of the past, we can now see walls and tunnels dug by Canaanites, the potential remains of King David's palace, the pool of Siloam and more.

During the periods of the first and second temple, the City of David was part of greater Jerusalem. From the Middle Ages (eleventh century CE) when the walls were rebuilt, the area was excluded. It was not until the arrival of western explorers that it was rediscovered.

Today, though it is still outside the old city walls built by Suleiman the Magnificent in the 16th centruy CE, the City of David has become an attraction for hundreds of thousands of visitors every year.

I invite you to discover its corners, tunnels and energy, which perhaps inspired King David as he composed many of his psalms. This is the place where he met and temporarily went crazy for Bathsheba and fled from his own son, Absalom, where also the prophets both encouraged and exhorted the kings of the Bible.

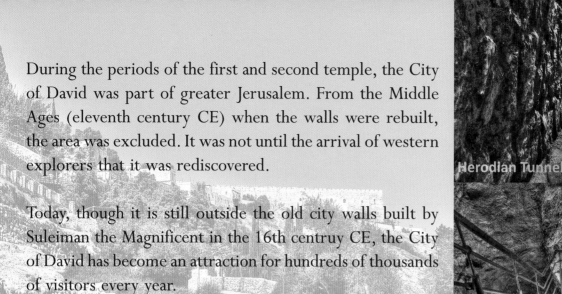

Herodian Tunnel

Canaanite Tunnel

Pool of Siloam

THE ARCHAEOLOGICAL PARK

Here, like the City of David, we can see how ancient civilizations left their footprint marks in the stone. Take the nineteenth century CE explorers who opened the doors to the past, and I cannot forget to mention archaeologists Charles Warren of England and, currently, Eilat Mazar of Israel. Also among them were many others whose contributions allow us today to walk among the park's ruins and appreciate its architecture. There we find walls, towers and rooms from the tenth century BCE, built by King Solomon.

We also see remains of other eras, namely Persian, Hellenistic and Hasmonean.

Byzantine Residence

Unarguably, the most predominate period displayed is that of Herod the Great, followed by remains of the Roman and Byzantine eras.

After the Muslim conquest, the Umayyad Caliphate's palaces were located in this area. The walls we see today, built by the Ottoman Turks, run through the archeological park.

The park also offers a small museum with a film and an excellent graphic of the temple area in ancient times.

Southern Steps

Solomonic Walls

Solomonic Royal Bakery

Mikvah (purification pool)

Byzantine Residence

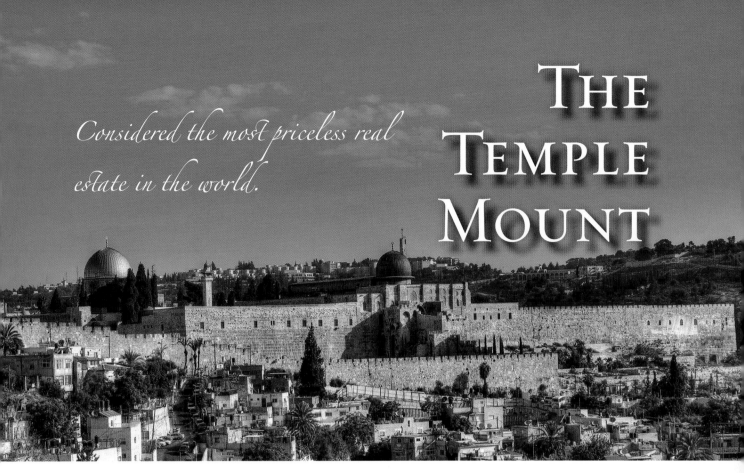

THE TEMPLE MOUNT

Considered the most priceless real estate in the world.

According to tradition, Jerusalem is the rock upon which God founded the world, the place where Father Abraham offered Isaac and where Jacob had his dream of the angels descending and ascending to heaven. Moreover, the Temple Mount is where Solomon built the First Temple, which in years to come was destroyed by the Babylonians. It is also the site of the Second Temple—built by those who returned from exile under the leadership of Zerubbabel—which Herod the Great extended (the artificial platform, approximately 300 x 500 meters, is on Mount Moriah). This is where Yeshua (Jesus) is believed to have been presented as a child.

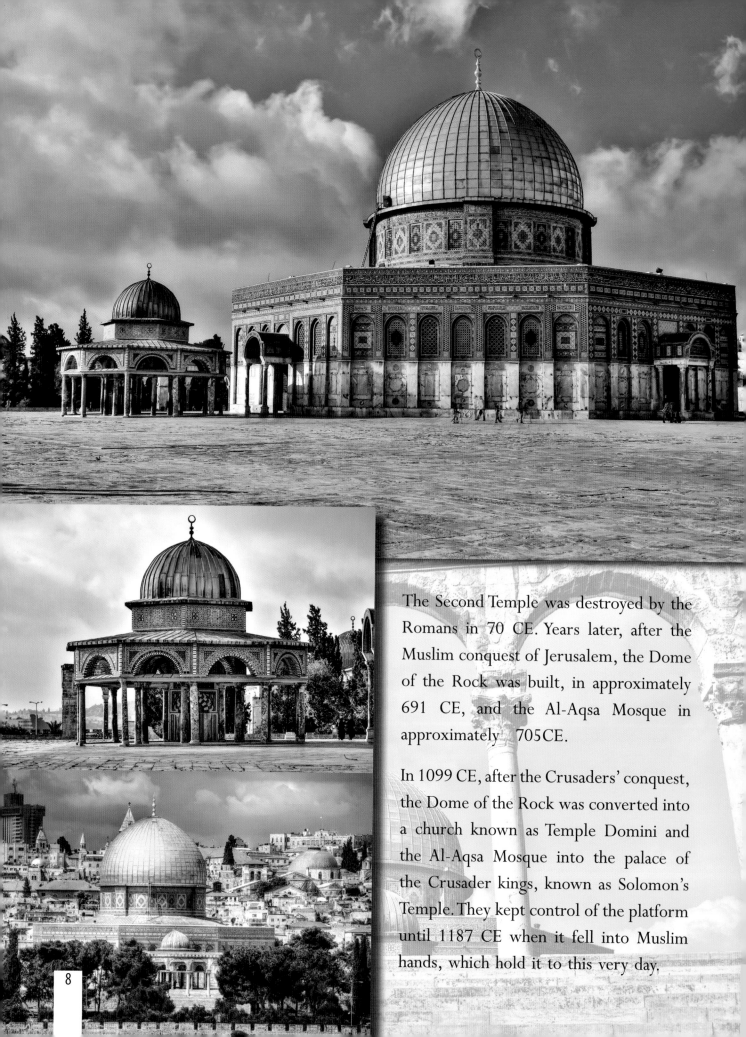

The Second Temple was destroyed by the Romans in 70 CE. Years later, after the Muslim conquest of Jerusalem, the Dome of the Rock was built, in approximately 691 CE, and the Al-Aqsa Mosque in approximately 705CE.

In 1099 CE, after the Crusaders' conquest, the Dome of the Rock was converted into a church known as Temple Domini and the Al-Aqsa Mosque into the palace of the Crusader kings, known as Solomon's Temple. They kept control of the platform until 1187 CE when it fell into Muslim hands, which hold it to this very day,

THE WESTERN WALL

The renowned Western Wall, built in 19 BCE under the supervision of Herod the Great, is almost 500 meters long, but you can only see part of it. The adjacent buildings were constructed in the fourteenth and fifteenth century CE, only leaving visible what we see today. And because of its proximity to the holiest site in Judaism, the wall is the prayer center for the Jewish people.

Due to its holiness, the whole present-day-plaza is a large open synagogue where prayer areas are designated for men and women separately. Clothing should be modest.

THE GATES OF JERUSALEM

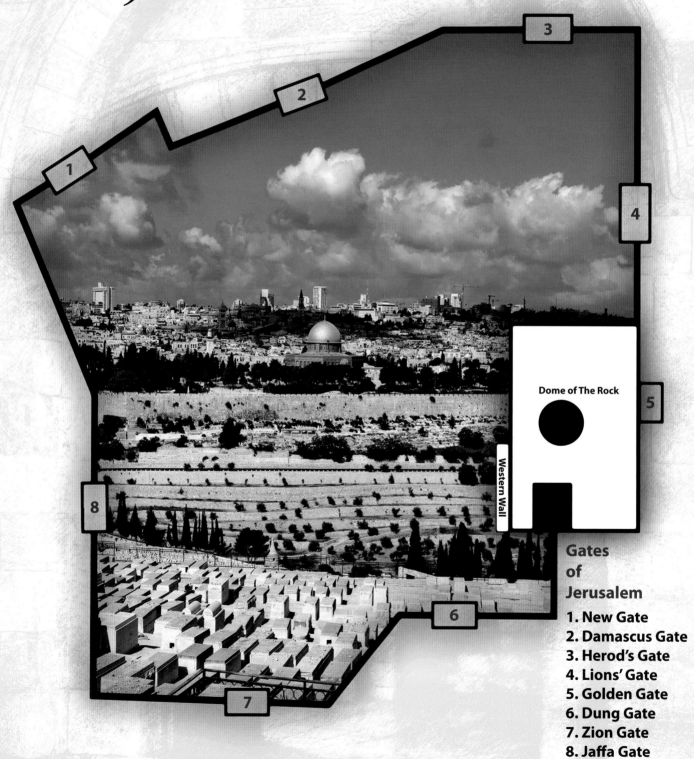

Dome of The Rock

Western Wall

Gates of Jerusalem

1. New Gate
2. Damascus Gate
3. Herod's Gate
4. Lions' Gate
5. Golden Gate
6. Dung Gate
7. Zion Gate
8. Jaffa Gate

New Gate

Located on the northwest side of the old city, it was the last gate to be built in 1887 CE. It leads into the Christian Quarter.

Located on the northern side of the old city, it was built in the sixteenth century CE by Suleiman the Magnificent. It is the most elaborate of all the gates. It leads into the Muslim Quarter.

Damascus Gate

Located on the
northern side of
the old city, its date
of construction
is unknown. It is
also known as the
Flower Gate.
It leads into the
Muslim Quarter.

HEROD'S GATE

Located on the east side of the old city, it was built in the sixteenth century CE by Suleiman the Magnificent. The door is also named after the martyr Stephen or called the Sheep Gate. It leads into the Muslim Quarter.

LIONS' GATE

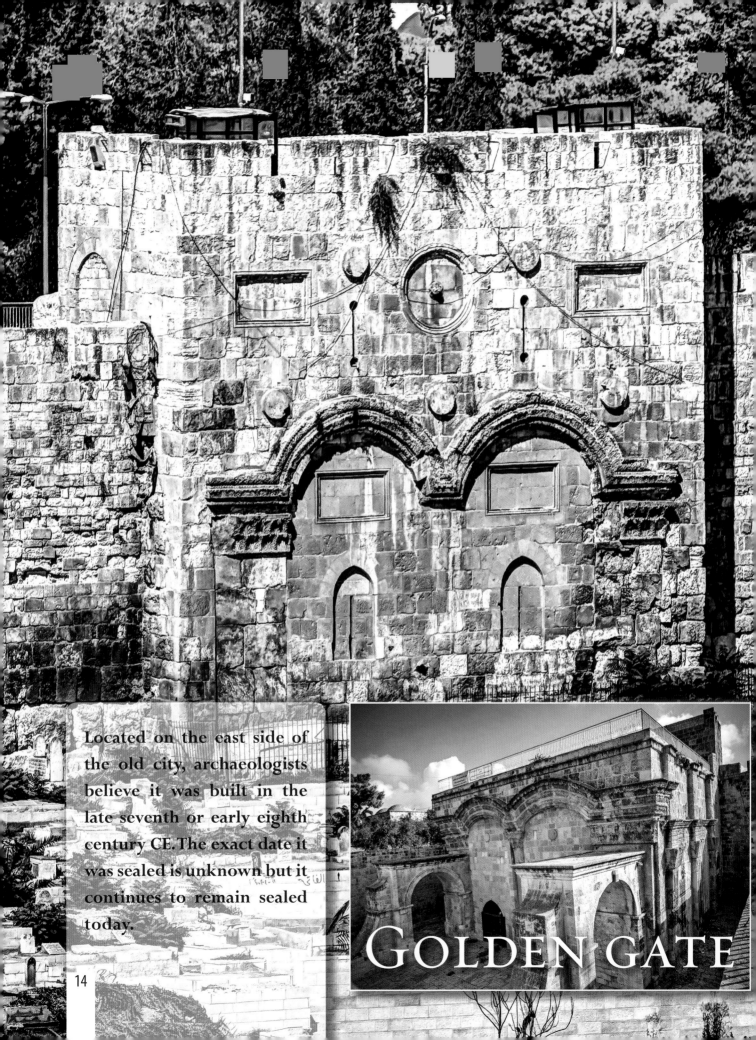

Located on the east side of the old city, archaeologists believe it was built in the late seventh or early eighth century CE. The exact date it was sealed is unknown but it continues to remain sealed today.

GOLDEN GATE

DUNG GATE

Located on the south side of the old city, it was originally built in the sixteenth century CE by Suleiman the Magnificent. Later it was modified during the Jordanian period in the nineteen fifties and the Israeli period in the late nineteen sixties.

It leads to the Western Wall, the Jewish and Muslim Quarters.

ZION GATE

Located on the south side of the old city, it was built in the sixteenth century CE by Suleiman the Magnificent.

It leads to the Armenian and the Jewish Quarters.

JAFFA GATE

Located on the west side of the old city, it was built in the sixteenth century CE by Suleiman the Magnificent.

It leads to the Christian and Armenian Quarters.

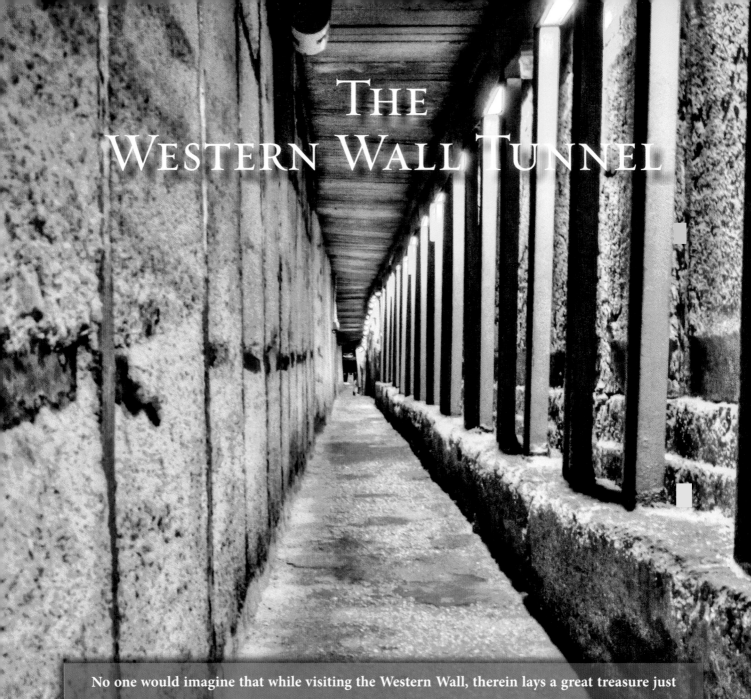

THE WESTERN WALL TUNNEL

No one would imagine that while visiting the Western Wall, therein lays a great treasure just under your feet. Arches and mega structures compose part of a tunnel that was created in the Middle Ages, forever sealing almost the 500 meters of the wall, which existed during the time of Yeshua (Jesus). On its surface are streets and residences of the Muslim Quarter of the old city. Visitors are invited to discover and explore this archaeological wonder.

Vaults of the Middle Ages

Largest Stone in the Western Wall

Warren's Gate

Herodian Street

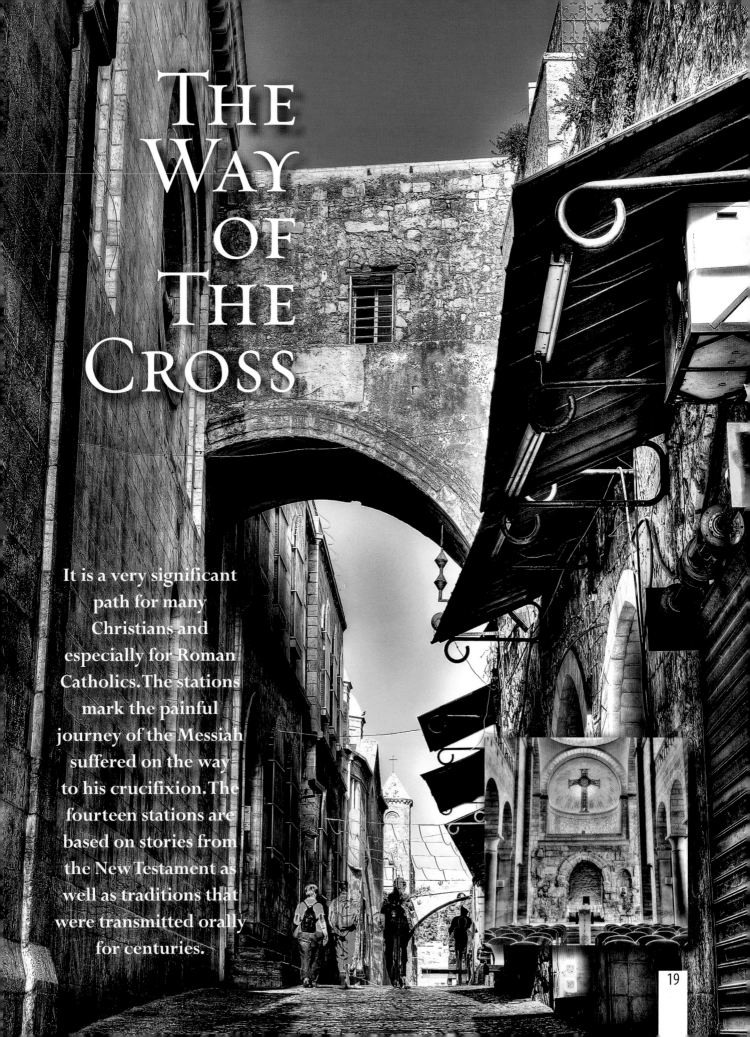

THE WAY OF THE CROSS

It is a very significant path for many Christians and especially for Roman Catholics. The stations mark the painful journey of the Messiah suffered on the way to his crucifixion. The fourteen stations are based on stories from the New Testament as well as traditions that were transmitted orally for centuries.

STATION I

Jesus is judged by Pontius Pilate.

Today this station is located in il-Umaria Arab school.

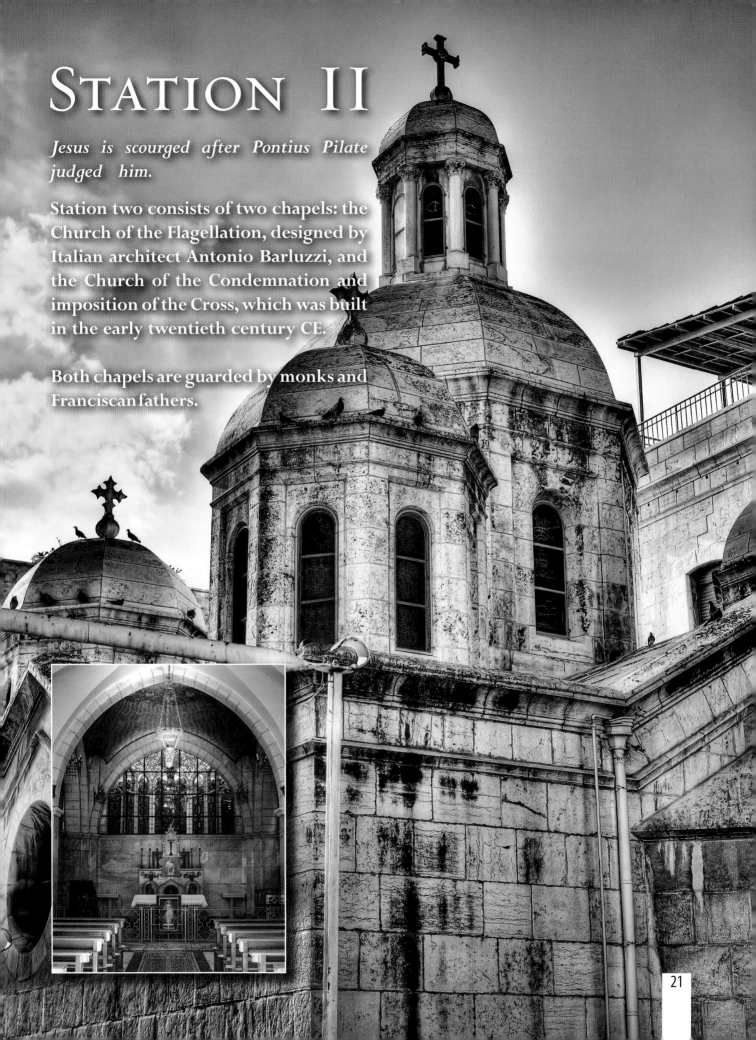

STATION II

Jesus is scourged after Pontius Pilate judged him.

Station two consists of two chapels: the Church of the Flagellation, designed by Italian architect Antonio Barluzzi, and the Church of the Condemnation and imposition of the Cross, which was built in the early twentieth century CE.

Both chapels are guarded by monks and Franciscan fathers.

STATION III

Jesus falls for the first time.
Armenian Catholic Patriarchate Chapel.

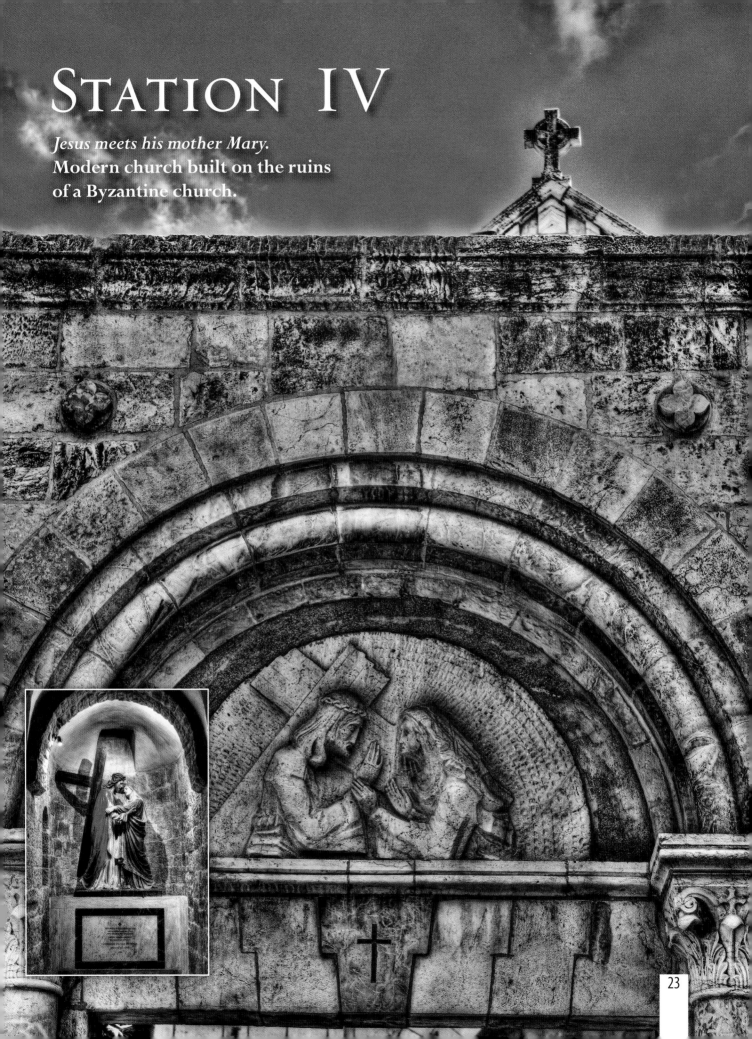

Station IV

Jesus meets his mother Mary.
Modern church built on the ruins of a Byzantine church.

STATION V

Franciscan Chapel.

Simon of Cyrene helps Jesus carry the cross.

V: SIMONI·CYRENAEO CRUX IMPONITUR. ST:

32

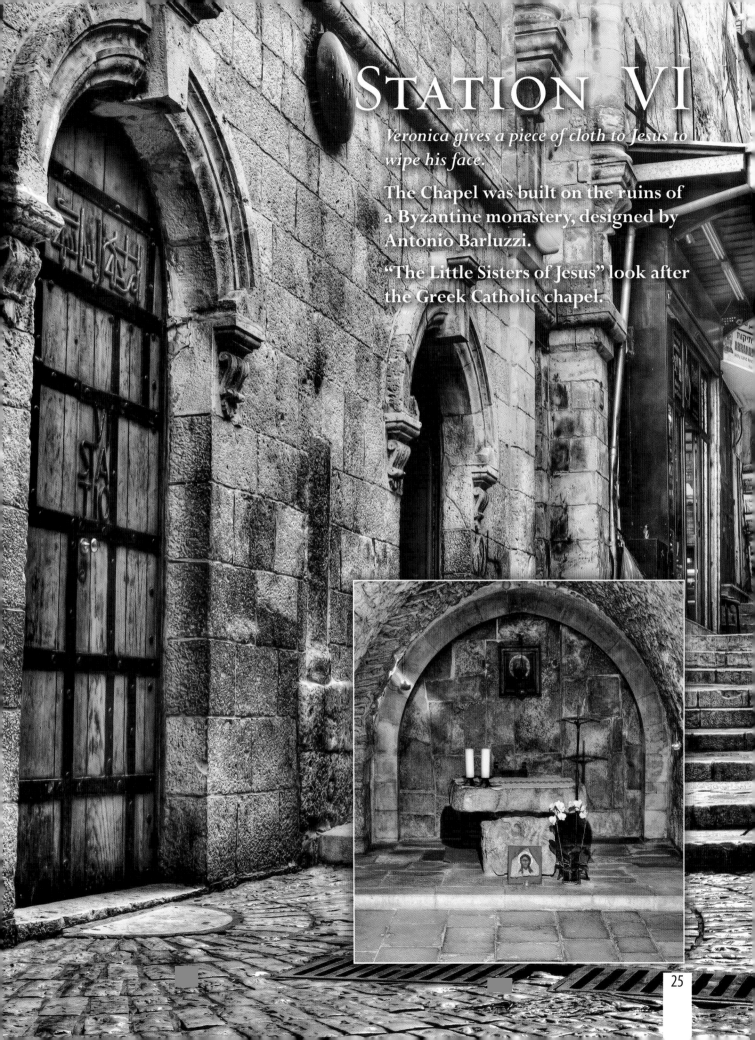

STATION VI

Veronica gives a piece of cloth to Jesus to wipe his face.

The Chapel was built on the ruins of a Byzantine monastery, designed by Antonio Barluzzi.

"The Little Sisters of Jesus" look after the Greek Catholic chapel.

STATION VII

Franciscan Catholic Chapel.
Jesus falls the second time

STATION VIII

Jesus turns his attention to the women of Jerusalem.

STATION IX

Jesus falls the third time.

IX

Station No. 9
St. HELEN COPTIC CHURCH

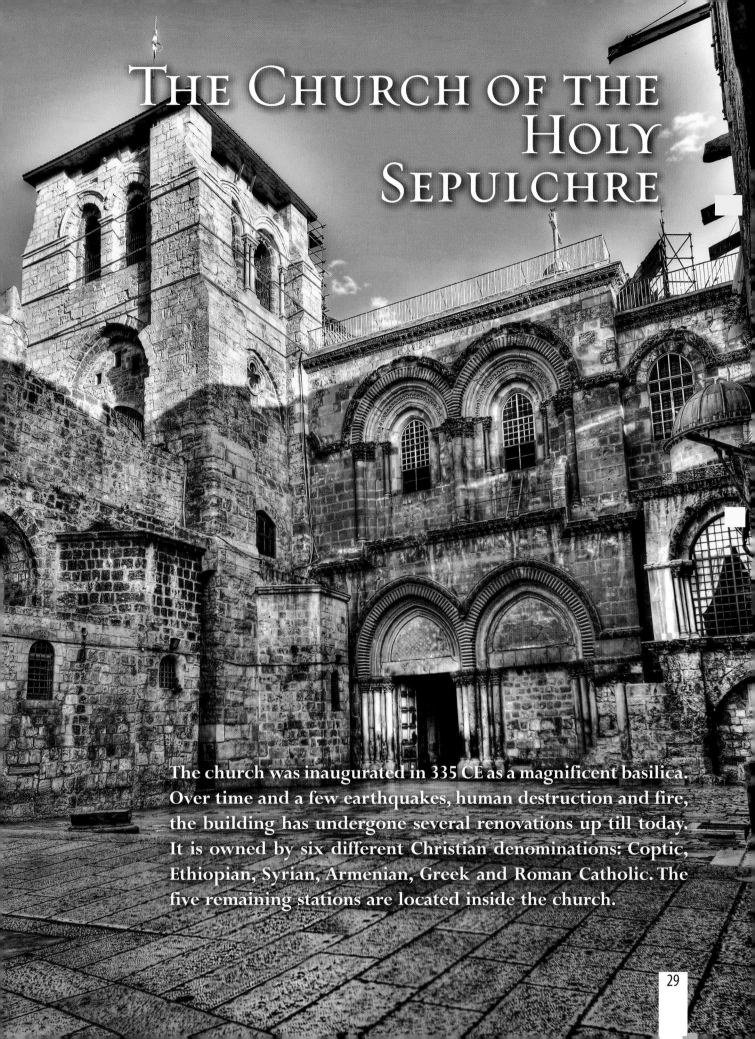

THE CHURCH OF THE HOLY SEPULCHRE

The church was inaugurated in 335 CE as a magnificent basilica. Over time and a few earthquakes, human destruction and fire, the building has undergone several renovations up till today. It is owned by six different Christian denominations: Coptic, Ethiopian, Syrian, Armenian, Greek and Roman Catholic. The five remaining stations are located inside the church.

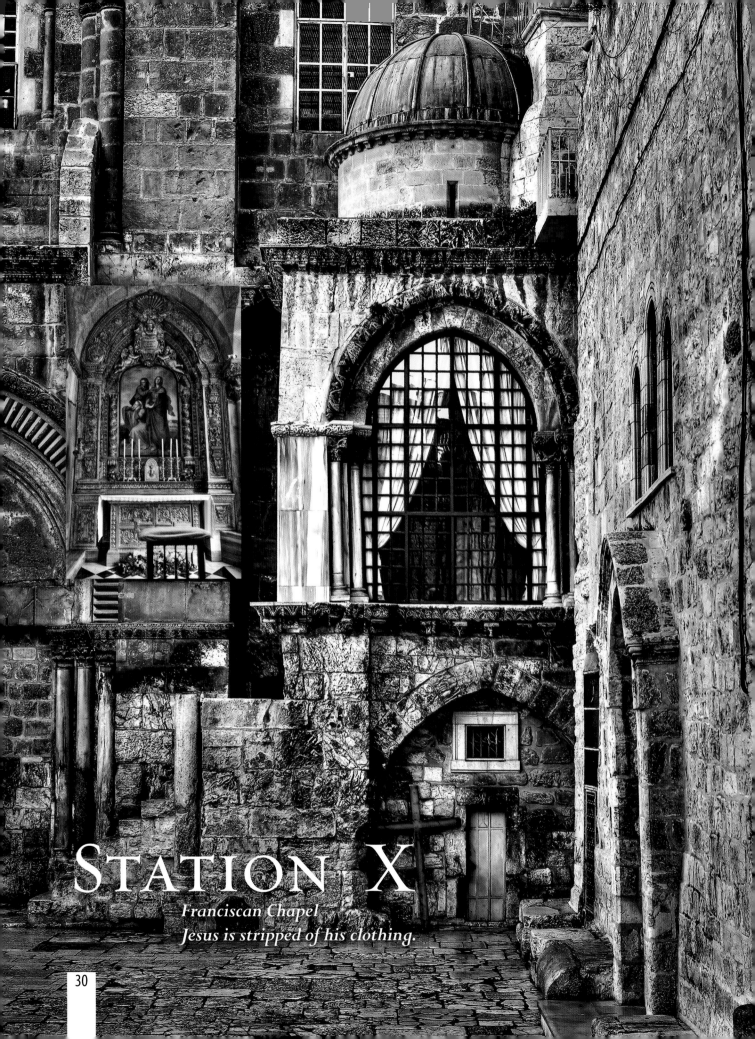

STATION X

Franciscan Chapel
Jesus is stripped of his clothing.

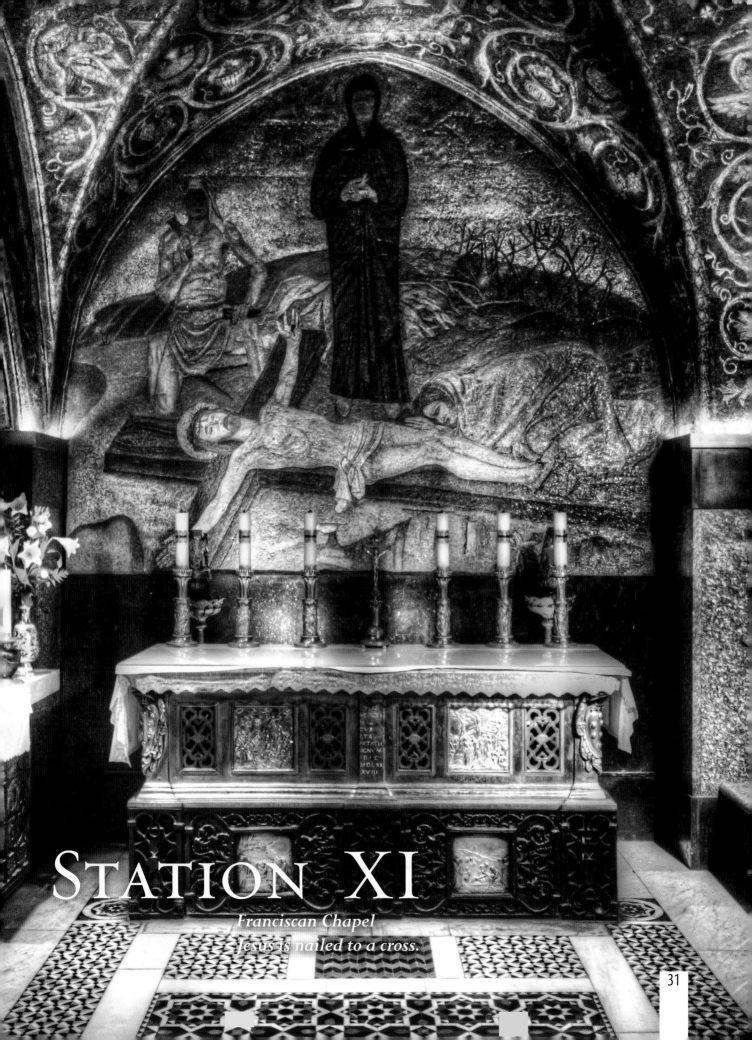

STATION XI

Franciscan Chapel
Jesus is nailed to a cross.

ΘΕΟΡΡΥΤΩ ЯΙΜΑΤΙ ΚΕΝΩΘΕΝΤΙ ΔΕΣΠΟΤΑ ΧΡΙΣΕ

STATION XII

Greek Orthodox Chapel
Jesus dies on the cross.

STATION XIII

Franciscan Altar
Jesus is handed over to his mother Mary.

Jesus is buried and resurrected.

Mosaic Depicting Jesus' Death and Burial

The Stone of Unction

The Chapel of St. Helena

Inside the Tomb of Jesus

St. Anne's Church

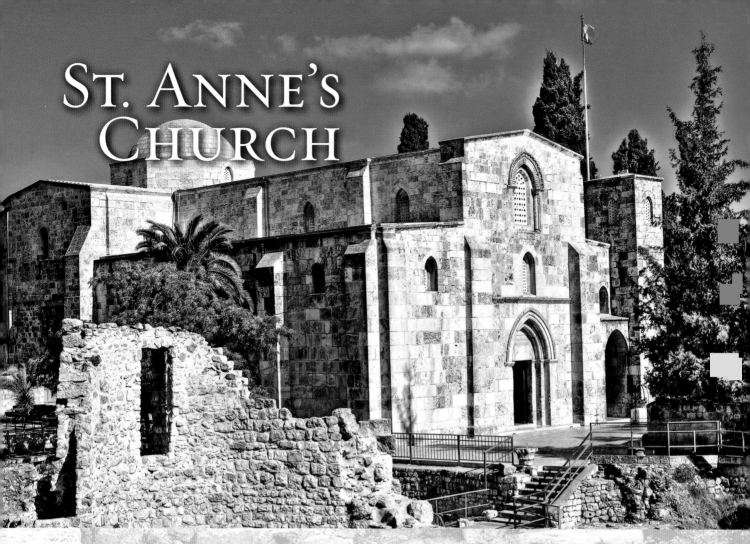

In the Gospel of John we read about a pool of water with eight porticoes, which lay outside the walls during the first century CE. It was believed that from time to time an angel from heaven came and stirred these waters and the first one to immerse himself was healed of all his ailments. The Bible tells of a paralytic man lying there whom Jesus called and commanded to walk. During the time of the Byzantine Christians, a basilica was erected there to commemorate this miracle by Jesus. However it was destroyed between the years 614 CE and 628 CE and today we see only its ruins.

In addition to this, and according to the Catholic tradition, this is the birthplace of Mary, the mother of Jesus.

LITHOSTROTOS

Lithostrotos in Greek, Gabbatha in Aramaic
"The Stone Pavement"

Roman Pavement

Underneath the convent of the Sisters of Zion, there lies a great archaeological jewel, which according to Christian tradition is the place where the Roman soldiers divided Jesus' garments. Below this floor is a large pond dating back to the days of the Hasmoneans and Herod the Great, which used to provide water for the Tower of Antonia. In the second century CE the Emperor Hadrian rebuilt the city and one of the forums (free markets) of the city in this area.

Roman Game

Roman Vaults over Herodian Moat

THE CITADEL

Located in the northwestern part, together with the famous "tower of David", the citadel is now a museum dedicated to the history of this great city, from its earliest inhabitants through the Renaissance to the state of Israel.

Herod the Great built his grand palace here and protected it with three strong towers. The first was named Miriam after one of his wives, the second was Phasael after his brother and the third Hippicus, after his best friend. Today we can appreciate the remains of one of these 3 towers.

The Crusaders also used the premises as their palace and built trenches and defense systems surrounding it. Suleiman the Magnificent built the façade you see today and the bridge.

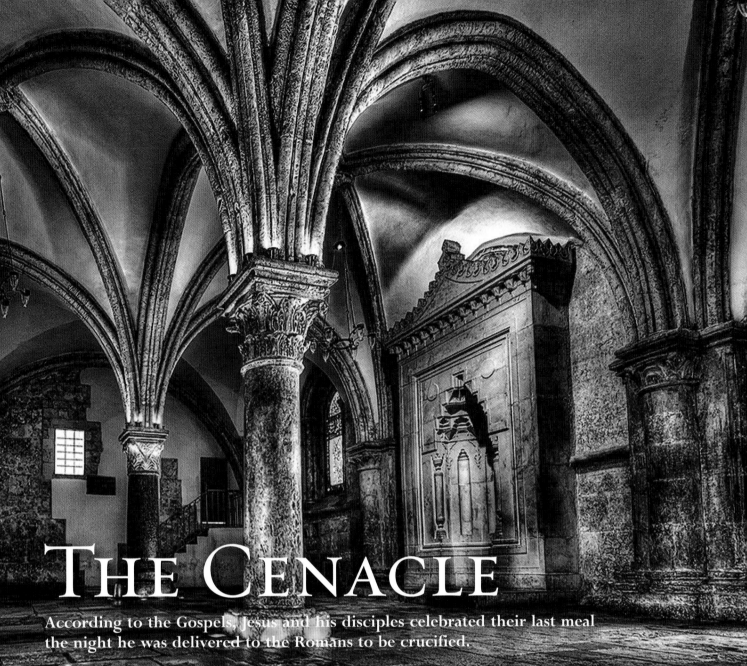

THE CENACLE

According to the Gospels, Jesus and his disciples celebrated their last meal the night he was delivered to the Romans to be crucified.

The early Christians recognized this site on Mount Zion as the congregation of the Apostles. By the fourth century CE there was a community of believers who met in this area, known as the Church of the Apostles. By the end of the fifth century CE a magnificent church was built next to the little one, known as Hagia Sion. This church was destroyed by the Sassanians in 614 CE and later rebuilt by the Crusaders in the twelve century CE; as the Church of St. Mary on Mount Zion.

After the fourteenth century CE, the Franciscans became the guardians of the holy places in the Holy Land. In the fifteenth century CE there was a dispute between the Franciscans and the Jews in the synagogue of the tomb of David. Both groups were expelled from the site by Suliman the Magnificent in the sixteen century CE and the enclosures were converted into a mosque .

Since the rebirth of Israel in 1948, Christians can return to the Upper Room to celebrate their rites as earlier Christians did for many centuries.

THE TOMB OF DAVID

The first time this synagogue was identified with the tomb of David was at the end of the tenth century CE and again in the twelfth century CE. Below the Upper Room there is a cenotaph as a reminder of the tomb of David.

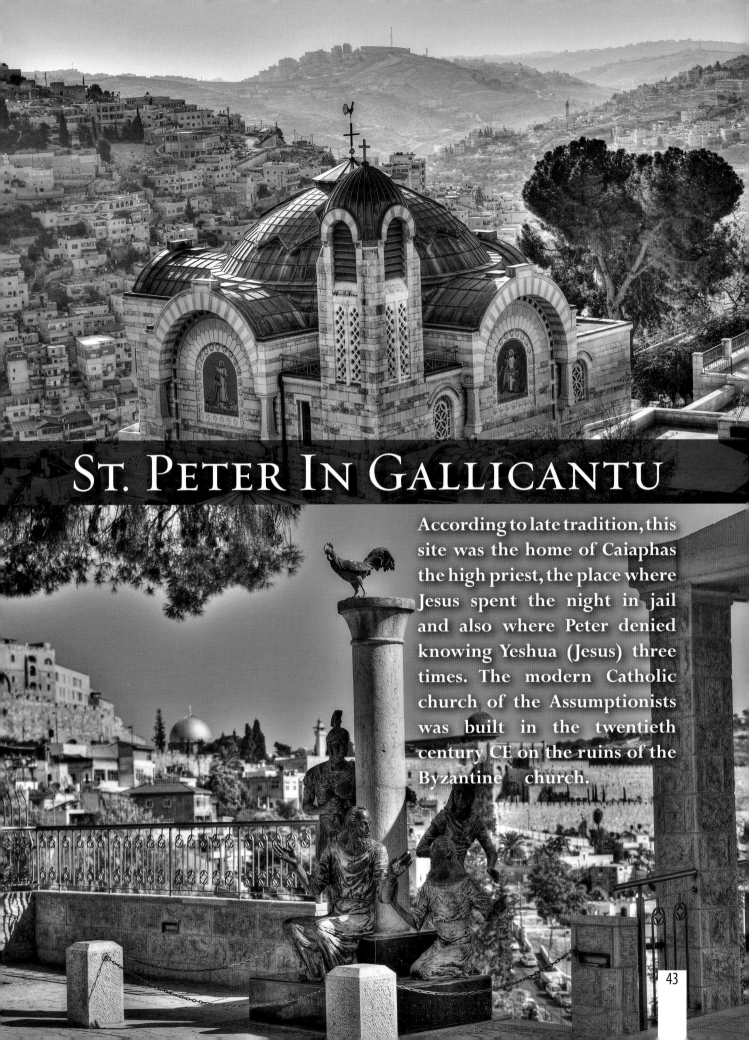

St. Peter In Gallicantu

According to late tradition, this site was the home of Caiaphas the high priest, the place where Jesus spent the night in jail and also where Peter denied knowing Yeshua (Jesus) three times. The modern Catholic church of the Assumptionists was built in the twentieth century CE on the ruins of the Byzantine church.

The Prison of Jesus

Built in the twentieth century on the ruins of the Byzantine church.

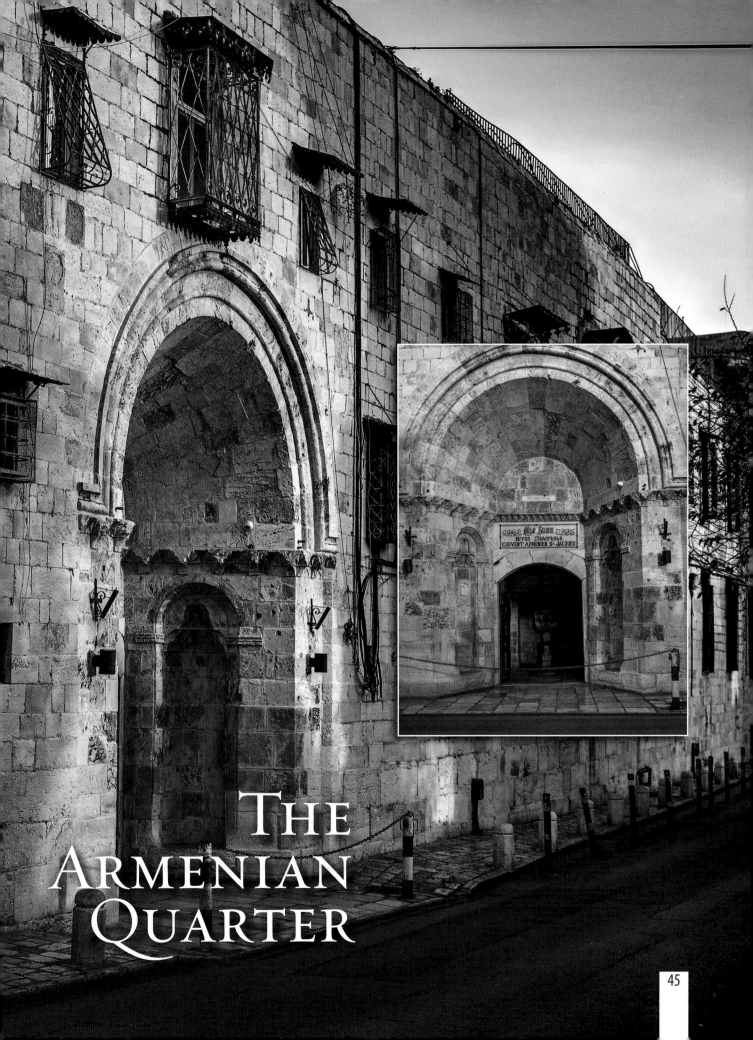

THE ARMENIAN QUARTER

The Armenians accepted Christianity as their official religion in the early fourth century CE, long before the Roman Empire adopted it as its official religion.

In the sixth century CE the Armenians began inhabiting the Holy Land and remain there to this day.

The Armenians are Eastern Christians with a monophysitic theological doctrine, holding that Jesus had only one nature, which is either divine or a synthesis of divine and human. They, along with other Eastern Christians, were excommunicated by the church in the council of Chalcedon in the fifth century CE.

Their main cathedral is dedicated to two saints, James the apostle and James the brother of Jesus. Today a few hundred still live in the old city.

The Armenian quarter is like a village within the Old City, containing a school, a cathedral, a monastery, craft shops and restaurants.

The Christian Quarter

It consists of various denominations including Catholic Christians, Greek Christians, Copts, Ethiopian Christians and Syrian Christians. These last four denominations represent the Eastern Orthodox Church, which is not under the leadership of the pope in Rome.

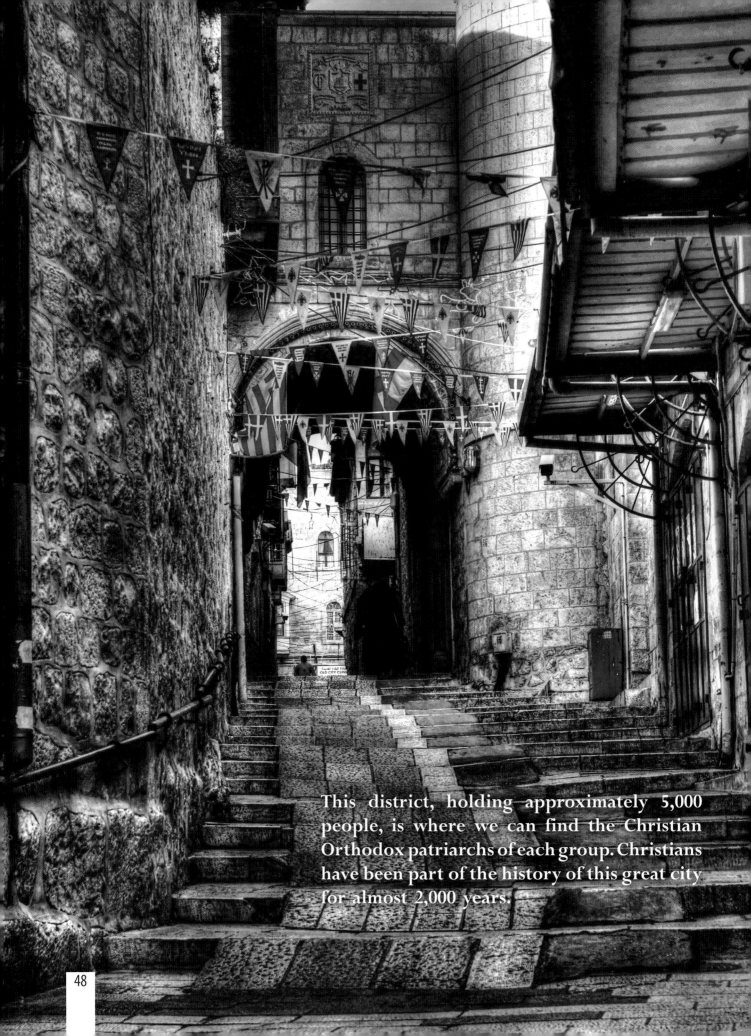

This district, holding approximately 5,000 people, is where we can find the Christian Orthodox patriarchs of each group. Christians have been part of the history of this great city for almost 2,000 years.

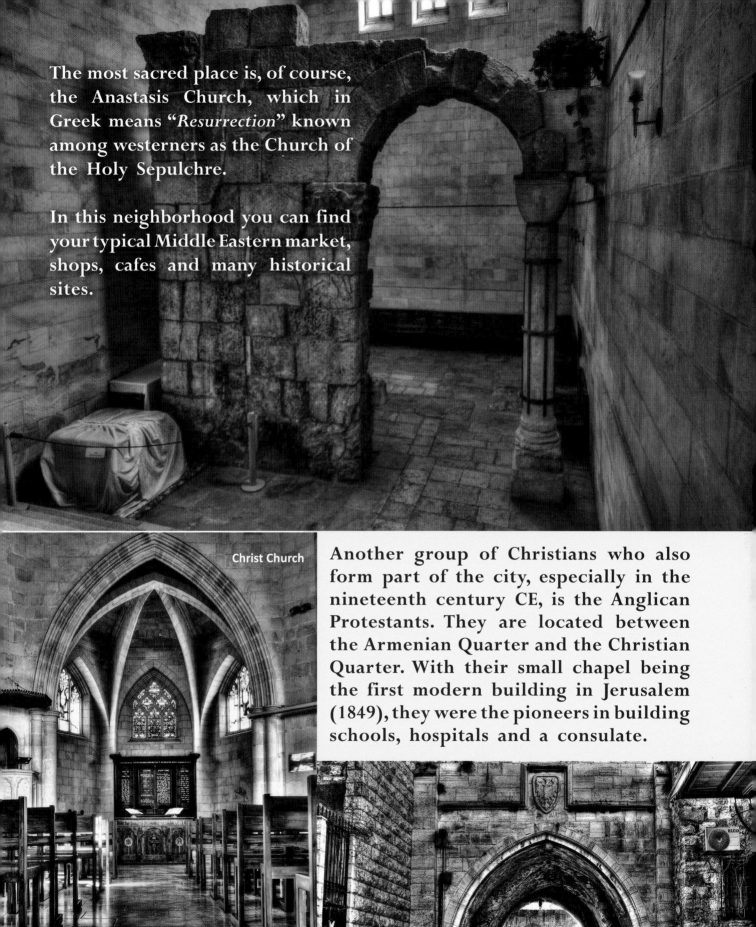

The most sacred place is, of course, the Anastasis Church, which in Greek means "*Resurrection*" known among westerners as the Church of the Holy Sepulchre.

In this neighborhood you can find your typical Middle Eastern market, shops, cafes and many historical sites.

Christ Church

Another group of Christians who also form part of the city, especially in the nineteenth century CE, is the Anglican Protestants. They are located between the Armenian Quarter and the Christian Quarter. With their small chapel being the first modern building in Jerusalem (1849), they were the pioneers in building schools, hospitals and a consulate.

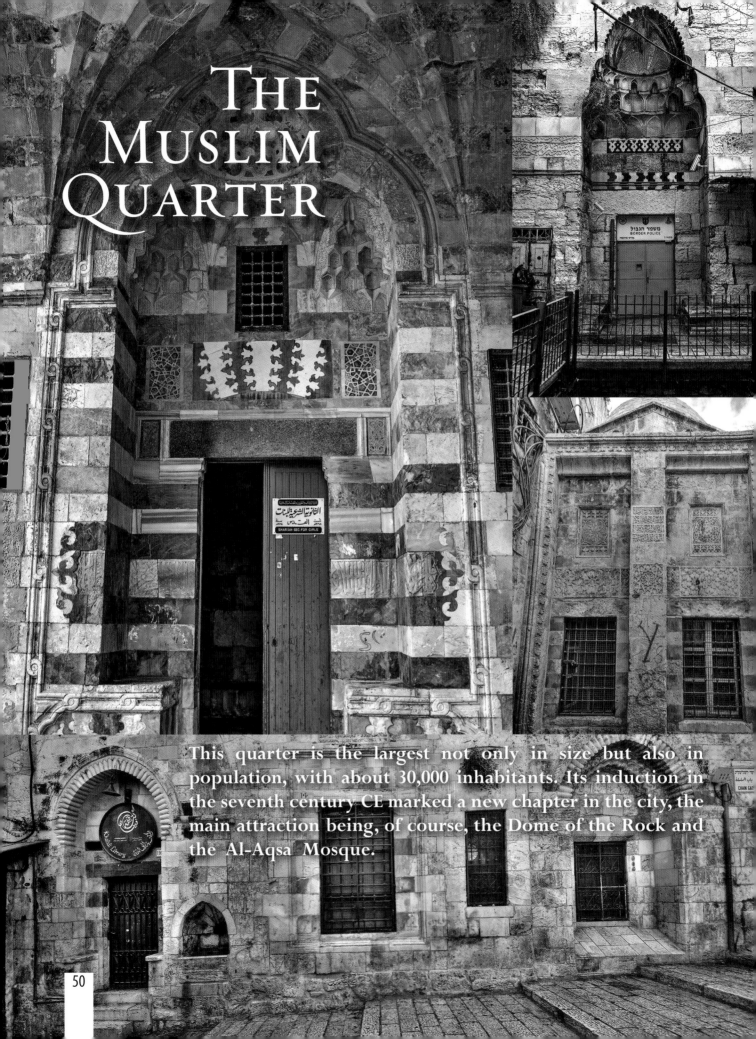

THE MUSLIM QUARTER

This quarter is the largest not only in size but also in population, with about 30,000 inhabitants. Its induction in the seventh century CE marked a new chapter in the city, the main attraction being, of course, the Dome of the Rock and the Al-Aqsa Mosque.

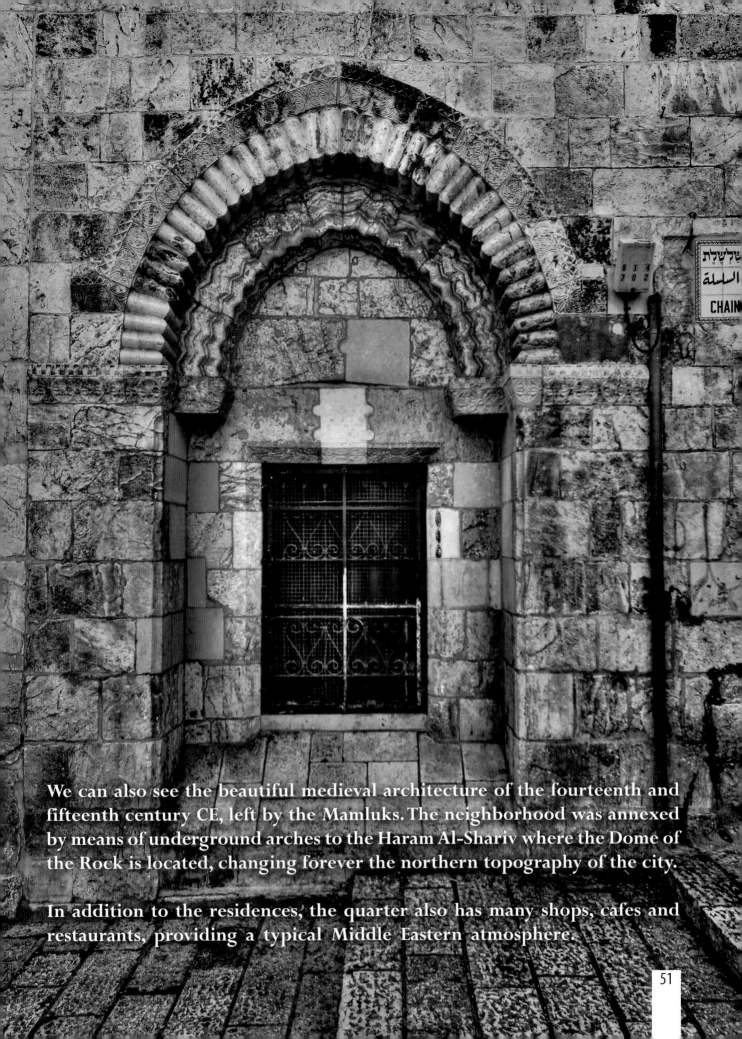

We can also see the beautiful medieval architecture of the fourteenth and fifteenth century CE, left by the Mamluks. The neighborhood was annexed by means of underground arches to the Haram Al-Shariv where the Dome of the Rock is located, changing forever the northern topography of the city.

In addition to the residences, the quarter also has many shops, cafes and restaurants, providing a typical Middle Eastern atmosphere.

THE JEWISH QUARTER

The Jewish Quarter has moved throughout the old city since the city's destruction in 70 CE and the second revolt in 132 CE. Its present location dates from the sixteenth century CE to the present day.

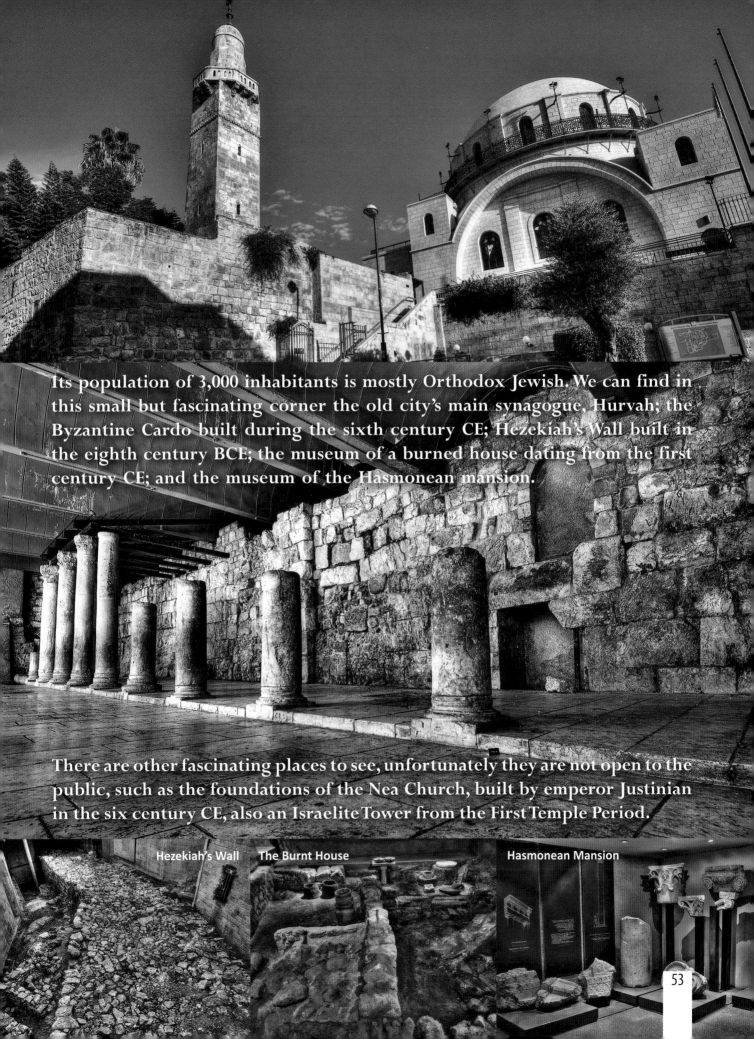

Its population of 3,000 inhabitants is mostly Orthodox Jewish. We can find in this small but fascinating corner the old city's main synagogue, Hurvah; the Byzantine Cardo built during the sixth century CE; Hezekiah's Wall built in the eighth century BCE; the museum of a burned house dating from the first century CE; and the museum of the Hasmonean mansion.

There are other fascinating places to see, unfortunately they are not open to the public, such as the foundations of the Nea Church, built by emperor Justinian in the six century CE, also an Israelite Tower from the First Temple Period.

Hezekiah's Wall   The Burnt House   Hasmonean Mansion

THE MOUNT OF OLIVES

The Mount of Olives is part of a ridge that divides the desert and the forest areas of Judea. It is located east of the old city of Jerusalem and the Kidron Valley separates the two. The Mount of Olives has many biblical references, which include Jesus' final week as well as his second coming.

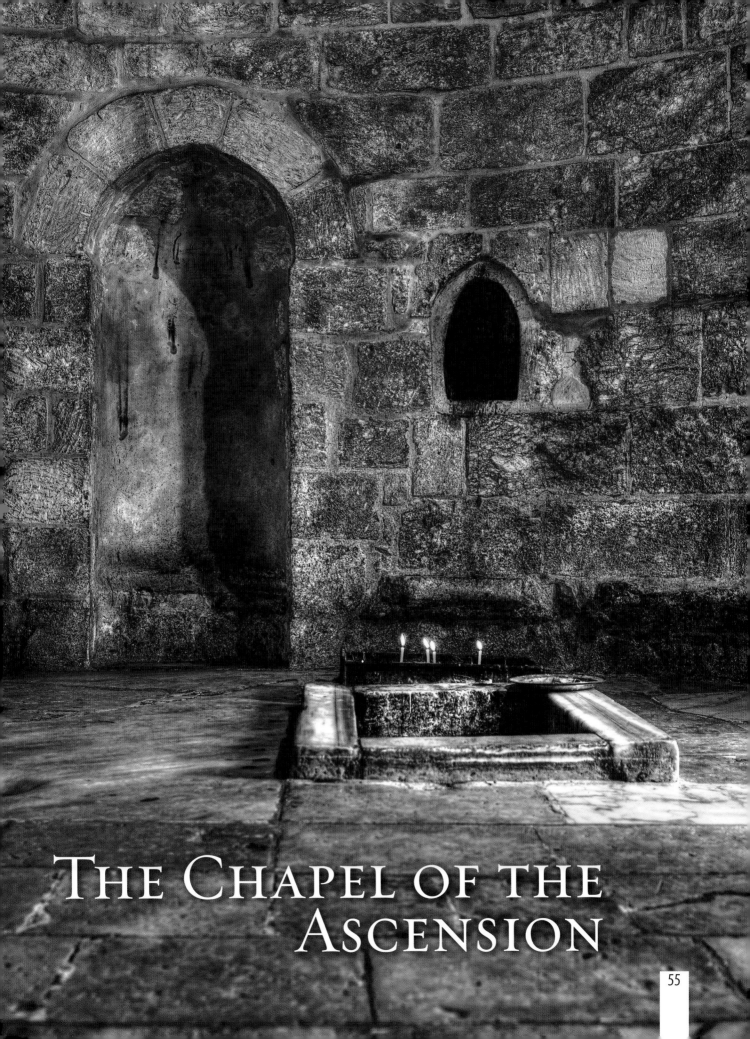

THE CHAPEL OF THE
ASCENSION

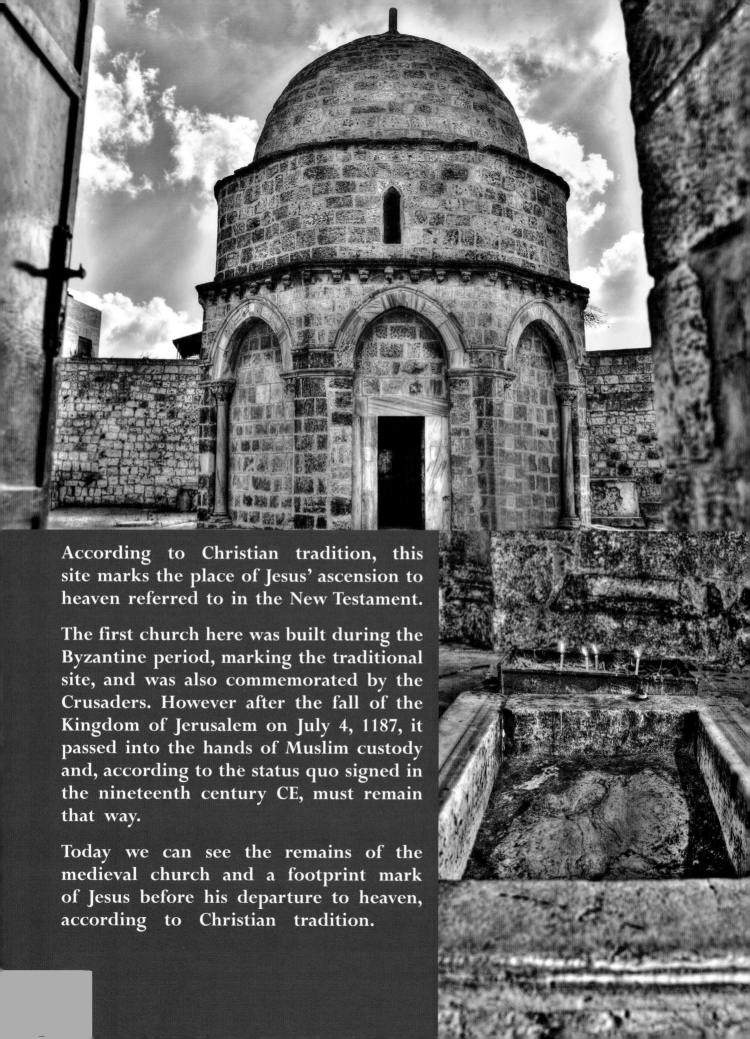

According to Christian tradition, this site marks the place of Jesus' ascension to heaven referred to in the New Testament.

The first church here was built during the Byzantine period, marking the traditional site, and was also commemorated by the Crusaders. However after the fall of the Kingdom of Jerusalem on July 4, 1187, it passed into the hands of Muslim custody and, according to the status quo signed in the nineteenth century CE, must remain that way.

Today we can see the remains of the medieval church and a footprint mark of Jesus before his departure to heaven, according to Christian tradition.

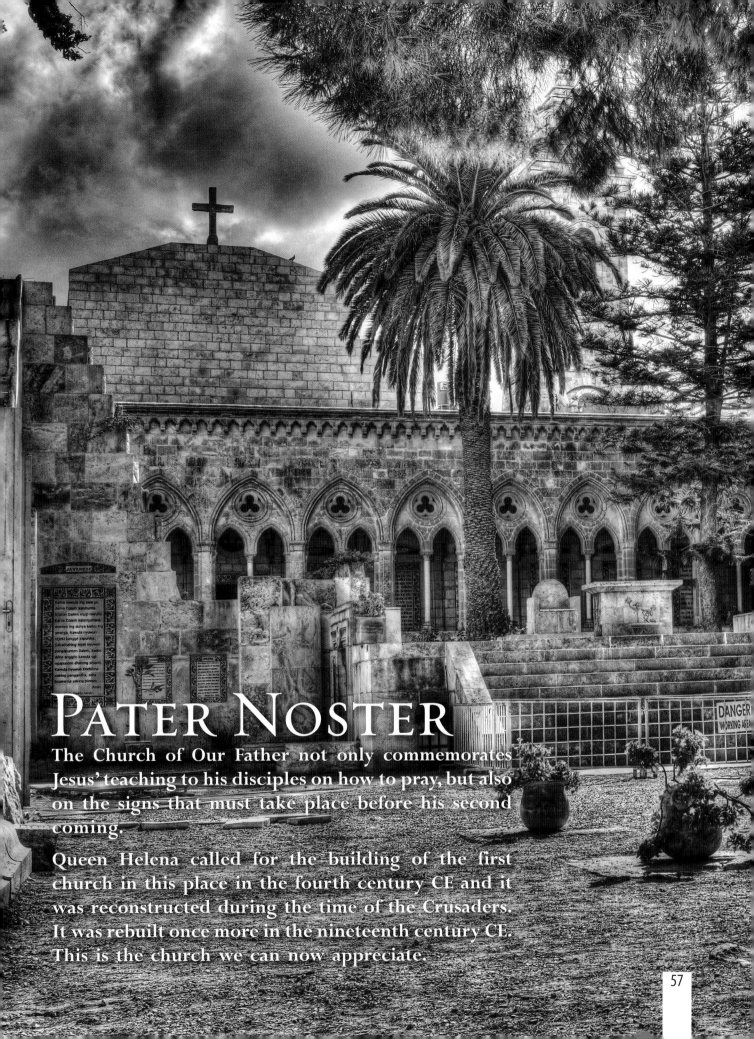

PATER NOSTER

The Church of Our Father not only commemorates Jesus' teaching to his disciples on how to pray, but also on the signs that must take place before his second coming.

Queen Helena called for the building of the first church in this place in the fourth century CE and it was reconstructed during the time of the Crusaders. It was rebuilt once more in the nineteenth century CE. This is the church we can now appreciate.

DOMINUS FLEVIT

This holy place captivates and draws us with her magic, spirituality, beauty and spectacular panoramic view of the city. We can imagine Jesus and his disciples as they took in this view at the triumphal entry the last week of his ministry.

The site commemorates Jesus weeping over Jerusalem, hence the name of the place, Dominus Flevit, "the Lord wept."

The chapel was built in the twentieth century by the Italian architect Antonio Barluzzi on the ruins of a church from the time of the Byzantines, which was destroyed in the seventh century CE.

Ancient Necropolis

GETHSEMANE

The church is also known as the Church of the Agony or the Church of All Nations, marking the last hours Jesus spent with his disciples the night he was arrested and taken to the religious authorities.

Here Jesus spends the most difficult moments of his ministry, surrendering his own will for that of his Father. Such was his agony that he sweat blood, and later was betrayed by one of his own disciples and abandoned by the rest of his followers.

Thus the Byzantines built the first Christian church here in the fourth century CE, which was destroyed in the seventh century CE to be rebuilt again by the Crusaders in the twelfth century CE.

Later in the twentieth century, the Franciscans rebuilt it under the direction of Italian architect Antonio Barluzzi.

THE GROTTO OF GETHSEMANE

The cave at the foot of the Mount of Olives is considered, according to Christian tradition, to be the place where Jesus spent his last night with his disciples before he was betrayed by Judas, one of his disciples.

In the fourth century CE, the natural cave was converted into a chapel and adorned with a mosaic floor. Later, tombs were dug in the Byzantine and even medieval periods.

From the late fourteenth century CE until today, the Franciscans remain its custodians.

THE TOMB OF MARY

According to the tradition of the Eastern Church, Mary, the mother of Jesus, died on Mount Zion and was brought to rest in this place where, after three days, her body ascended to heaven. Thus in the fifth century CE a church was built here to commemorate this event.

The church then went through a series of destructions and reconstructions over the ages. In the seventh century CE, it was destroyed by the Sassanians then rebuilt by the Crusaders. Later on the church was also rebuilt by Saladin and the Franciscans. Todays its custodians are the Greek Orthodox and the Armenians. They were said to find the tomb of QueenMelisende, Baldwin III's mother, who was one of the monarchs that reigned in Jerusalem during the Crusader period in the twelfth century CE. Also according to Christian tradition this is the location of the tomb of Joseph the father of Yeshua (Jesus).

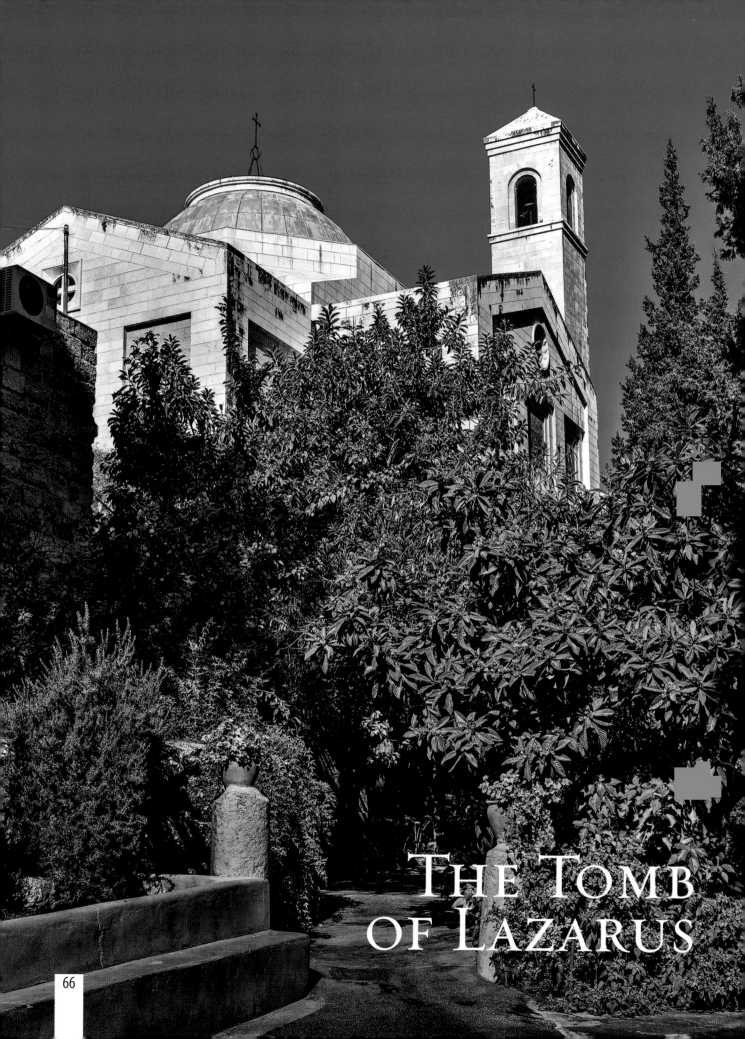

THE TOMB
OF LAZARUS

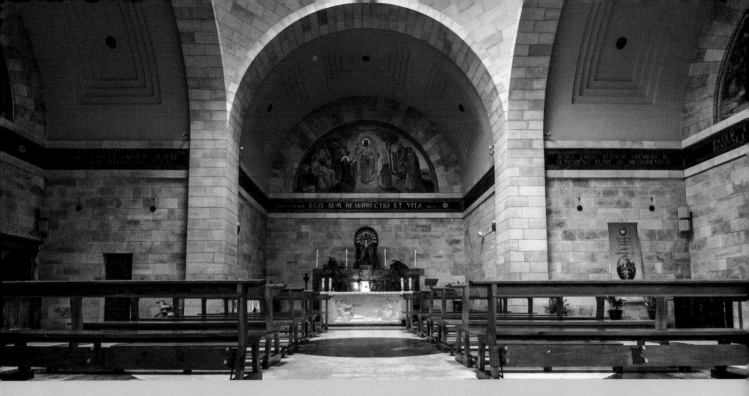

Lazarus, Martha and Mary were friends of Jesus and supported his ministry. The Gospels tell us that at one time Lazarus fell sick and died, but was resurrected from the dead by Jesus.

For this reason, in the fourth century CE, the Byzantine Christians built the first church here to commemorate the miracle of the resurrection of Lazarus. In the sixth century CE it was extended, but regrettably suffered the same disaster as the other churches in the Sassanian invasion of the seventh century CE.

The church was later rebuilt in the twelfth century CE by the Crusaders but damaged by the return of Muslims in the area.

The present church was built by the Franciscans and designed by Italian architect Antonia Barluzzi.

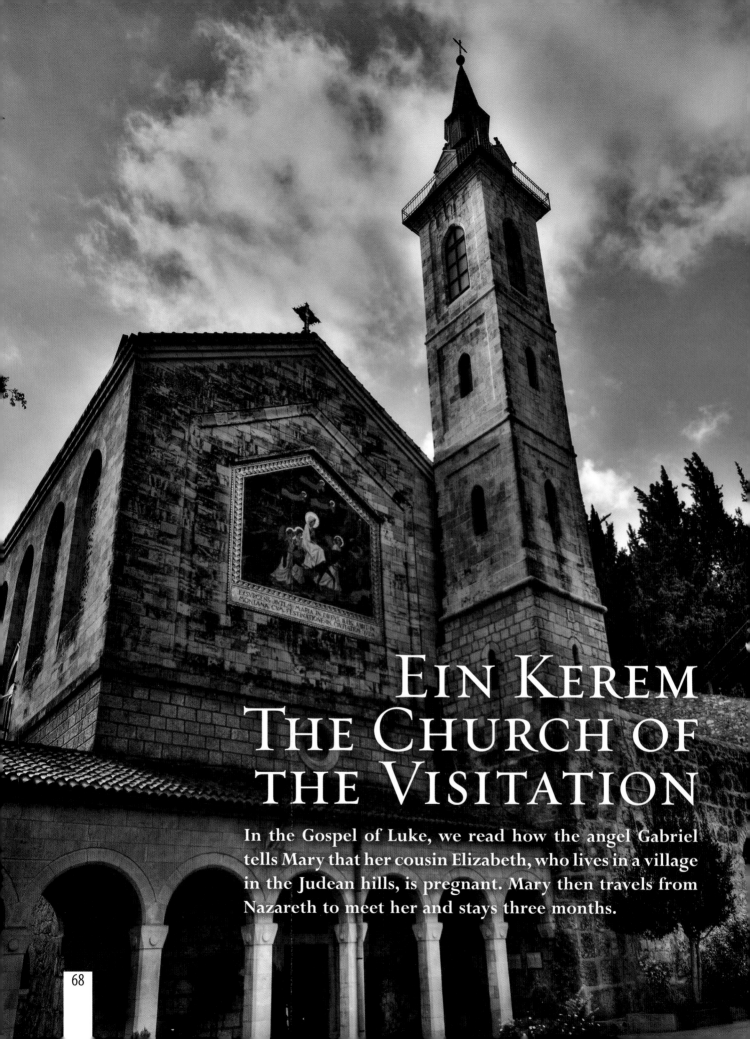

Ein Kerem
The Church of the Visitation

In the Gospel of Luke, we read how the angel Gabriel tells Mary that her cousin Elizabeth, who lives in a village in the Judean hills, is pregnant. Mary then travels from Nazareth to meet her and stays three months.

According to Christian tradition, Ein Kerem was identified as the village where Elizabeth and her husband, Zechariah, lived during the summer. For this reason, at the end of the fourth century CE, the first Byzantine church was built here, which was later abandoned in the seventh century CE. The church was revived during the Middle Ages under the Crusaders but, sadly, was destroyed. In the seventeenth century CE, the Franciscans succeeded to buy the land and rebuilt the church once more in the twentieth century CE.

In the courtyard is the Magnificat in several languages as well as a depiction of Mary meeting her cousin Elizabeth.

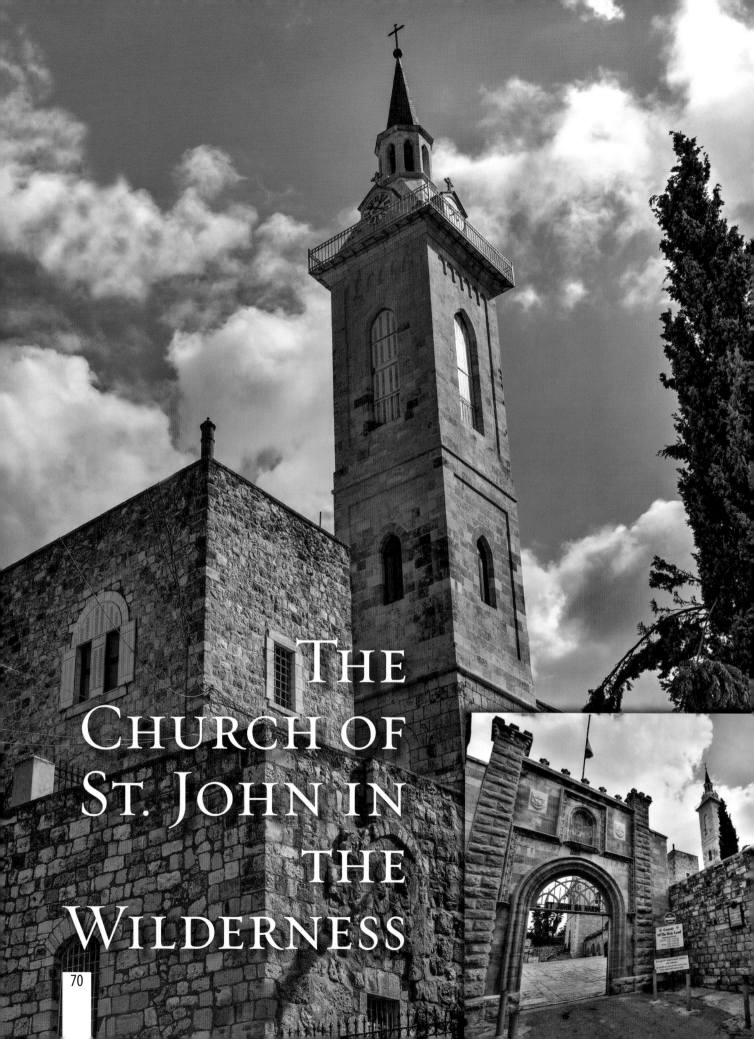

The Church of St. John in the Wilderness

According to Christian tradition, this shrine celebrates the place where John the Baptist was born.

The Byzantines built the first church here on ruins from the first century CE. However, in the sixth century CE, it was destroyed during the Samaritan revolt.

Later with the arrival of the Crusaders, the church was rebuilt. Yet it suffered the same fate in the hands of the Muslims when they returned to this region.

Thanks to their dedication, the Franciscans were able to rescue many sacred sites as they bought land in the seventeenth century CE. With the help of the Spanish crown, they built the monastery in the nineteenth century CE and the church in the twentieth century CE.

In the courtyard we can see the Benedictus in twenty-four languages, the prayer of Zechariah the father of John, as we read in Luke 1:67-79.

OPENING HOURS	Summer (April-September)	Winter (October-March)
Armenian Cathedral of St. James Tel. 02-6282331	Mon - Fri. & Sun 6.30 - 7.30 Daily 15.00 - 15.40 Sat. 6.30 - 9.30	Mon-Fri & Sun. 6.30 - 7.30 Daily 15.00 - 15.40 Sat 6.30 - 9.30
Ascension Mosque, Mount of Olives Mobile: 050 6780671 ; 054 5261092	Ring the bell	Ring the bell
City of David (Tel. 02-626-8700 or *6033) **And The Archaeological Park**	08:00-19:00 Friday 08:00-16:00 Shabbat Closed	08:00-17:00 08:00-14:00
Basilica of the Holy Sepulchre Tel. 02-6267000	5.00 - 21.00	4.00 - 19.00 25th December the Basilica opens at 8.00 am.
Bethany St. Lazarus Tel. 02-2799291	8.00 - 11.45 / 14.00 - 18.00	8.00 - 11.45 / 14.00 - 17.00
Bethfage Tel. 02-6284352	8.00 - 12.00 14.00 - 17.00	8.00 - 12.00 14.00 - 16.30
Cenacle- Last Supper Room	8.00 - 18.00	8.00 - 18.00
Christian Information Center Tel. 02-6272692	Mon - Fri 9.00 - 17.30 Sat 9.00 - 12.30 Sun closed	Mon - Fri 9.00 - 17.30 Sat 9.00 - 12.30 Sun closed
Dominus Flevit Tel. 02-6266450 / 6266456	8.00 - 11.45 14.00 - 17.00	8.00 - 11.45 14.00 - 17.00
Dormition Abbey - Mount Zion Tel. 02-5655330	Mon - Sat 9.00 - 17.30 Sun 11.30 - 17.30	Mon - Sat 9.00 - 17.30 Sun 11.30 - 17.30
Ecce Homo - Lithostrotos Tel. 02-6277292 Entrance fee: 9 NIS, 6 NIS	8.00 - 17.00 Good Friday for prayer only.	8.00 - 17.00
The Western Wall Tunnel Tel. 02-627-1333	Sunday-Thursday: 07:00-evening (depending on reservations) Fri. and on the Jewish eve festival: 07:00-12:00	Shabbat Closed
Ein Kerem, St. John's Church Tel. 02-6323000	8.00 - 12.00 / 14.30 - 17.45	8.00 - 12.00 / 14.30 - 16.45
Ein Kerem, St. John's in the Desert Tel. 02-6416715	8.00 - 18.00	8.00 - 17.00
Ein Kerem, Visitation Church Tel. 02-6417291	8.00 - 11.45 / 14.30 - 18.00	8.00 - 11.45 / 14.30 - 17.00
Flagellation Church, Via Dolorosa Tel. 02-6270444	8.00 - 18.00	8.00 - 17.00

The Wohl Archaeological Museum and the Burnt House in the Jewish Quarter Tel. 02-629-3448	Sunday-Thursday 09:00-17:00 Friday 09:00-13:00	Closed on Shabbat
Al-Haram Al-Sharif (Temple Mount)	Monday-Thursday 08:30-11:30 13:00-14:30	07:30-10:30 12:30-13:30
Garden Tomb Tel: 02 539 8100	9.00 am - 12.00 / 14.00 - 17.30; Sun. closed Groups have to book before	9.00 am - 12.00 / 14.00 - 17.30; Sun. closed Groups have to book before
Gethsemane Basilica Tel: 02-6266444	8.00 - 18.00	8.00 - 17.00
Gethsemane Grotto Tel: 02-6266444	8.30 - 12.00 / 14.30 - 17.00 (Sun. & Thurs. till 16.00)	8.30 am - 12.00 / 14.30 - 17.00 (Sun. & Thurs. till 16.00)
The Citadel Tel 02-626-5333	Sun-Th 09:00-16:00 (Aug 09:00-17:00) Fr 09:00-14:00 (Aug 09:00-14:00)	Shabbat 09:00-16:00 Aug 09:00-17:00
Lutheran Church of the Redeemer Tel: 02-6266800 Entrance fee to tower & museum: 15 NIS	10.00 - 17.00 Sun. closed	10.00 - 17.00 Sun. closed 25th, 26th December, 1st, 6th January closed.
Pater Noster Church - «Eleona» Mt. of Olives Tel: 02-6264904 Entrance: 8 NIS	8.30 - 12.00 / 14.30 - 16.30 Sun. closed	8.00 - 12.00 / 14.30 - 16.30 Sun. closed 25th December closed.
St. Alexander's Church (Judgment Gate) Tel: 02-6274952 Entrance fee: 5 NIS	9.00 - 18.00	9.00 - 18.00
St. Ann's Basilica & Pools of Bethesda Tel: 02-6283285, Entrance 8 NIS	8.00 - 12.00 / 14.00 - 18.00	8.00 - 12.00 / 14.00 - 17.00 Sunday, 8th December: Church opens only in the afternoon: 14:00 - 17:0
St. Mark's Syrian Church Tel: 02-6283304, 052 5090478	9.00 - 17.00 Sun. 11.00 - 16.00	7.00 - 16.00 Sun. 11.00 - 16.00
St. Mary Magdalene Tel: 02-6284371	Tuesday & Thursday 10.00 - 12.00	Tuesday & Thursday 10.00 - 12.00
St. Peter in Gallicantu Tel: 02-6731739 Entrance 7 NIS	8.30 - 17.00 Sunday closed	8.30 - 17.00 Sunday closed 25th December, 1st January closed.
Tomb of Mary Tel: 02-6284613	5.00 - 12.00 / 14.30 - 17.00	6.00 - 12.00 / 14.30 - 17.00

OPENING HOURS

BIBLICAL REFERENCES

Psalms: 14; 26; 42;48;75;84;87;95;127;133;134;137;146;147;1
50; Song of Ascent:122

Gn 14, 18. Melchizedek King of Salem

2 Sam 5:1-12. Conquest by David

1 Kn 7:1-12. Construction of Solomon's palace

2 Sam 6:1-23 Political and religious capital of the kingdom

2 Kn 14:13. Joash (northern kingdom) attacks Jerusalem

Ne 3:1-38. Restoration of Jerusalem walls by Nehemiah

Lk. 21:20. Jesus foretells the destruction of Jerusalem

Ez 23; Is 62. Jerusalem represents the chosen people

Ps 76:3. God's Home

Nh 11:1 The Holy city

Isa 2:1-5;60 Meetings place of the nations

Is. 54:11-17;62. Vision of the New Jerusalem

Rv 21:2. The Holy City, the new Jerusalem at the end of time

THE TEMPLE MOUNT AND THE CITY OF DAVID

2 Sam 7:1-17. David wishes to build a house for God

2 Sm 24:18-25. David buys the threshing-floor of Arunah

1 Kn 5 & 6 Construction of Solomon's temple

1 Kn 8. Dedication of the temple.

Is 6:1-8. Vision of the prophet Isaiah in the temple

2 Kn 11:1-20. Murder of queen Athalia of Judah outside the temple

2 Kn 12:1-22. Reparation under king Johoash

2 Kn 22:1-20. The book of the law found in the temple

Ez 8:1-18. Vision of Ezekiel on idolatry

Ez. 10:18-22. The glory of the Lord leaves the temple

2 Kn. 25. Destruction of the temple by Nebuchadnezzar 586 BCE

Ez 40 & 44. Vision of the future temple: the New Jerusalem

Ez. 4:24 & 6:1-18. Reconstruction and dedication of the temple
515 BCE

1 Mac 1:20-42. Plunder of the temple by Antiochus Epiphanes

Lk 1:5-25. The birth of John the Baptist foretold

Lk 2:22-38. Presentation of Yeshua in the temple

Lk 2:40-52. Finding Yeshua in the temple

Lk4:9-13. Pinnacle of the temple-temptation of Yeshua

Mt 21:12-17. Expulsion of the dealers from the temple also
Mk 11:15-19; Lk 19:45-46; Jn 2:13

Jn 5:14. Yeshua meets the cured man from Bethesta

Jn 5:19-30. "The Son of God can do nothing by Himself"

Jn 7:1-53. Taxes to Caesar, looking for the glory of God

Jn 8:1-11. The adulterous woman

Jn. 8-12-21. I am the light of the world

Jn. 8:51-59. Discussions with the Judeans

Jn 10:22-39. My sheep hear my voice

Jn 11:45-53. The plot against Yeshua

Mt 21:23. What authority have you for acting like this?

Mk 12:41-44. The widow's mite

Mt. 24:1-25 Prophecy of the ruin of the temple

Mt 27:3-10. Judas returns 30 silver coins

Mt 27:52. Veil of the temple torn in two

Acts 3. Cure of a lame man by Peter

Acts 21:15; 22; 23:22. Paul in the temple

Gal 4:26. The Jerusalem above is free and is our mother

1 kn 1:28-55. Solomon receives the royal unction

1 Ch 11:4-9. Joab enters into Jerusalem by the tzinor,
also 2 Sm 5:6-10

2 Kn 20:20 . King Hezekiah digs a tunnel, also 2 Ch 32:30;

2 Sm 5:7; Ch 11:5. The City of David fortress of Zion

2 Sm 6:10-12. The ark of God in the citadel of David

Is. 8:18. YHWH dwells on mount Zion

Is 2:3. They will come and shout for joy on the heights of Zion

1 Mac. Nicanor on Mount Zion

ENROGEL

2 Sm 17:17-23. David send spies

2 Sm 18:1-18. Revolt and death of Absalom

POOL OF SILOAM

Is. 7:3. Isaiah sent Ahaz

Is. 22:9-11. Oracle against the city

Jn. 9 The cure of the man born blind

Lk 13:4-5. The tower of Siloam

THE MOUNT OF OLIVES – GETHSEMANE

2 Sm 15:30-32. David leaves Jerusalem trying to flee from
Absalom

1 Kn 11:7-8. Solomon builds a palace for his foreign wives.

2 Kn 23:12-13. Destruction of the altars by Josias

Ez 14:3-4 the Glory of the Lord rose to leave the city and
paused on the mountains to the east of the city

Zc 14:3-4. YHWH will fight against these nations as he fights
in the day of battle

Jn 18:2. Yeshua had often met his disciples there

Mt 26:30-56. The Agony of Yeshua in Gethsemane, also Mk
14; Lk 22

Lk 24:50. The Ascension of Yeshua., also Acts 1:4:12

Mk 13:3. Yeshua announces the destruction of the temple

Lk 22:39. He then left to make his way as usual to the Mount
of Olives